Test 2 Multiplication and division

Fill in the missing number for each of these multiplication and division problems. Check your answers with your number-spotter.

7.6   x   10   =   _____

45   x   7   =   _____

$\dfrac{25}{5}$ =   _____

84   ÷   12   =   _____

240   ÷   8   =   _____

75   x   9   =   _____

133   x   3   =   _____

41.8   x   5   =   _____

48.6   ÷   10   =   _____

$\dfrac{108}{9}$ =   _____

212   x   4   =   _____

725   ÷   25   =   _____

612   ÷   3   =   _____

15.3   x   100   =   _____

81   x   7   =   _____

642   ÷   6   =   _____

Test 3 Up to a million

Write the correct value, in words, for each of these questions.
Try them all, then check your answers with the number-spotter.

What is the value of...
the 2 in 182 374? _____

the 7 in 475 821? _____

the 6 in 621 439? _____

the 8 in 553 068? _____

the 1 in 1 243 254? _____

the 2 in 3 407 129? _____

the 5 in 25 121 029? _____

Now try writing these values in figures.

seventy-eight thousand, three hundred
and four _____

two hundred and thirty-two thousand
and twenty-six _____

six million, twelve thousand,
five hundred and seven _____

four hundred and three thousand,
seven hundred and one _____

twelve million, fifty-six thousand,
two hundred and twenty _____

Test 4 Estimates

Which number do you think the arrow is pointing to on each of these lines? Check your answers with your number-spotter.

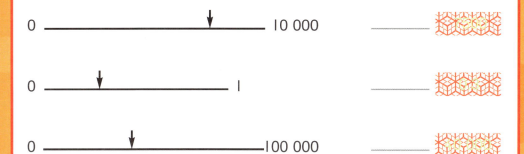

About what proportion of this cake has been sold?

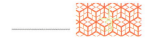

This jar holds 3000 beans when full. Here 1200 beans are left in the jar.

What proportion is this?

What is that as a percentage?

Test 5 Multiples of 10 to 1000

Complete these questions. Write your answers in the spaces.
Then check them with your number-spotter.

35   x   100   =   _____

$\dfrac{1}{1000}$ of 8200   =   _____

$\dfrac{1}{100}$ of 24   =   _____

4.5   x   1000   =   _____

_____   x   100   =   7

_____   ÷   1000   =   1.1

63   ÷   _____   =   0.63

5.7   x   _____   =   570

How many…

£100 notes in £22 000?   _____

£10 notes in £6500?   _____

£1 coins in £7150?   _____

10p coins in £470?   _____

£10 notes in £37 000?   _____

Tins of beans at 36p each are in packs of 10.
10 packs are put in a box.
10 boxes are put in a crate.
How much is…

1 crate of beans?   _____

1 box of beans?   _____

100 crates of beans?   _____

Test 6 World time

Fill in the correct time for each question using the chart below, then check your answers with your number-spotter.

Times around the World						
London	Paris	Hong Kong	Tokyo	Sydney	San Francisco	New York
12.00 noon	1.00pm	8.00pm	9.00pm	10.00pm	4.00am	7.00am

When it is 10.00am in London, what time is it in…

Sydney? _____

San Francisco? _____

New York? _____

Tokyo? _____

Paris? _____

Hong Kong? _____

When it is 3.00am in Tokyo, what time is it in…

London? _____

Paris? _____

Sydney? _____

Hong Kong? _____

New York? _____

San Francisco? _____

Test 7 More or less than

Add on or take away to find an answer for each of these questions. Write your answers in the spaces, then check them with your number-spotter.

What is…

100m more than 7500m? _____

1000p more than £1.12? _____

10l less than 2308l? _____

1000kg less than 4872kg? _____

1000mg more than 370mg? _____

100g more than 21 075g? _____

1000km less than 12 204km? _____

1000ml more than 71ml? _____

1000g more than 9708g? _____

100m less than 72 092m? _____

1000p less than £510.64? _____

1000kg more than 19 045kg? _____

100km more than 80 944km? _____

1000l more than 10 799l? _____

1000mg less than 20 765mg? _____

100ml less than 9005ml? _____

1000m more than 12km? _____

1000g less than 74kg? _____

Test 8 Fractions

Try these fraction questions. When you've filled in all your answers, check them with your number-spotter.

Circle the correct answers.

$\frac{1}{4}$ is equivalent to	$\frac{35}{100}$	$\frac{5}{20}$	$\frac{3}{8}$	$\frac{3}{12}$
$\frac{1}{2}$ is equivalent to	$\frac{7}{15}$	$\frac{2}{5}$	$\frac{5}{10}$	$\frac{25}{50}$
$\frac{2}{3}$ is equivalent to	$\frac{6}{9}$	$\frac{11}{15}$	$\frac{17}{30}$	$\frac{16}{24}$
$\frac{1}{5}$ is greater than	$\frac{3}{10}$	$\frac{3}{20}$	$\frac{23}{100}$	$\frac{5}{30}$
$\frac{3}{4}$ is less than	$\frac{5}{8}$	$\frac{7}{12}$	$\frac{13}{20}$	$\frac{21}{24}$

What is…

$\frac{1}{3}$ of £750 _____

$\frac{1}{5}$ of 200g _____

$\frac{3}{4}$ of 10 litres _____

$\frac{2}{3}$ of 1500m _____

$\frac{2}{5}$ of 10kg _____

$\frac{7}{8}$ of 240km _____

$\frac{3}{5}$ of 1000ml _____

Fill in the spaces to complete the table.

Fraction	Decimal	Percentage
$\frac{1}{5}$	0.2	_____
$\frac{7}{10}$	_____	70%
$\frac{23}{100}$	0.23	_____

Test 9 Rounding up and down

Round these numbers, writing each answer in the space provided. When you've tried them all, check your answers with your number-spotter.

Round these numbers to the nearest metre.

1275mm _____

1762mm _____

3156mm _____

Round these numbers to the nearest whole number.

0.702 _____

6.345 _____

10.805 _____

Round these numbers to the nearest kilometre.

72 890m _____

27 365m _____

14 486m _____

Round these numbers to the nearest 10 000.

71 326 _____

12 687 _____

132 743 _____

Round these numbers to the nearest tenth.

0.201 _____

0.835 _____

5.481 _____

Test 10 Negative numbers

Try these negative number problems. Write your answers in the spaces provided, then check them with your number-spotter.

−20 + 7 = _____

18 − 25 = _____

21 − 30 = _____

−4 + 12 = _____

−12 + 12 = _____

6 − 15 = _____

This graph shows temperatures over 5 days.

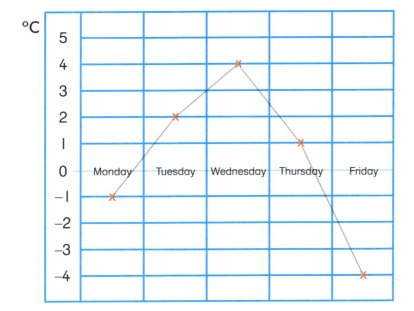

What was the temperature on Friday? _____

What was difference between Monday's temperature and Friday's temperature? _____

How much did the temperature rise between Tuesday and Wednesday? _____

How much did the temperature fall between Thursday and Friday? _____

Test 11 Shapes

Match one shape to each of the descriptions below. When you've filled in the answers, check them with your number-spotter. The first one has been done for you.

A
trapezium

B
parallelogram

E
square

F
kite

C
rhombus

D
rectangle

has two pairs of opposite sides which are equal and parallel but no right angles   B

has four right angles and two pairs of opposite sides which are equal   _____

has four equal sides and four equal angles   _____

has one pair of opposite parallel sides, one longer than the other   _____

has two pairs of equal, adjacent sides   _____

has four equal sides and two pairs of equal angles.   _____

Test 12 Sequences

Fill in the spaces to complete these sequences.
Check your answers with your number-spotter.

100   119   138   157   _____   _____   _____

65   80   95   110   _____   _____   _____

234   213   192   171   _____   _____   _____

1.7   2.2   2.7   3.2   _____   _____   _____

29   17   5   −7   _____   _____   _____

9.3   8.2   7.1   6.0   _____   _____   _____

−36   −25   −14   −3   _____   _____   _____

3.75   4.0   4.25   4.5   _____   _____   _____

Extend these patterns.

1   3   6   10   15   _____ _____ _____

4   9   16   25   36   _____ _____ _____

1   2   3   5   7   _____ _____ _____

Test 13 Multiples

Try these questions about multiples. Write your answers in the spaces provided, then check your answers with your number-spotter.

Circle the numbers that are multiples of...

12	25	36	42	60	80	95
3	129	247	384	401	523	
9	171	223	496	634	855	
4	427	684	733	804	946	
8	245	328	510	736	954	

If a line of beads is laid out in a pattern:
5 yellow, 4 red, 5 yellow, 4 red…

What colour is the 39th counter?   _____

What colour is the 70th counter?   _____

What position in the line is
the 15th red counter?   _____

What position in the line is
the 22nd yellow counter?   _____

14

Test 14 Money

Try these money problems, writing your answers in the spaces provided. Check your answers with your number-spotter.

Mark these items down to half price.

£25.98   ———————   £12.99

£58.64   ———————   £29.32

£288   ———————   £144

£744.40   ———————   £372.20

Share £840 420 between…

4 lottery winners   ———————   £210 105

6 lottery winners   ———————   £140 070

Total…

£45.12, £17.30 and £5.27   ———————   £67.69

£19.36, £123.90 and £7.04   ———————   £150.30

£24.70, £102.93 and £14.99   ———————   £142.62

If there are 1.7 US Dollars, 190 Japanese Yen and 1.6 Euros to £1, what is the cost of a car costing £6000 in…

Dollars?   —————————————   10 200 Dollars

Yen?   —————————————   1 140 000 Yen

Euros?   —————————————   9600 Euros

Test 15 Proportions

Try these ratio problems. Write your answers in the spaces provided, then check them with your number-spotter.

What proportion (fraction) of one ordinary year is…

one week?   _____ $\frac{1}{52}$

one day?   _____ $\frac{1}{365}$

May?   _____ $\frac{31}{365}$

What fraction of 1 litre is 510ml?   _____ $\frac{51}{100}$

What fraction of 1km is 727m?   _____ $\frac{727}{1000}$

What fraction of 1kg is 263g?   _____ $\frac{263}{1000}$

What percentage of £30 is £18?   _____   60%

What percentage of 5kg is 2kg?   _____   40%

What is 50% of 150?   _____   75

What percentage of 200m is 140m? _____   70%

What is 0.31 of £10.00?   _____   £3.10

What is 0.9 of 300g?   _____   270g

What is 0.64 of 200km?   _____   128km

What is 0.1 of 2l?   _____   200ml

Test 16 Which sign?

Make each of the following sums read correctly by adding the correct function sign from the list below. Check your answers with the number-spotter. The first one has been done for you.

$$+ \quad - \quad \times \quad \div \quad < \quad >$$

$\frac{7}{8}$	$>$	$\frac{3}{4}$		
99	____	11	=	9
125	____	4	=	500
321	____	487	=	808
750	____	255	=	495
$\frac{3}{4}$	____	$\frac{7}{12}$		
7.2	____	8	=	0.9
32	____	25	=	800
$\frac{2}{5}$	____	0.6		
0.7	____	5	=	3.5
2600	____	94	=	2506
190	____	2	=	95
477	____	68	=	545
0.14	____	0.9		
234	____	36	=	6.5
1571	____	292	=	1279

Test 17 Time

Use the train timetable below to answer these problems.
Write your answers in the spaces provided. Check them
with your number-spotter.

Leeds	08.40	09.05	10.05	11.25
Sheffield	09.20	09.55	10.55	....
Nottingham	09.45	10.20	11.20	11.40
Birmingham	10.55	11.30	12.30	12.50
Coventry	11.25	....	13.00	....
Oxford	12.20	12.55	13.55	14.10

When does the 08.40 from Leeds
arrive at Coventry?   _____

How long does it take the 10.55
from Sheffield to reach Oxford?   _____

How long does it take the 10.05
from Leeds to reach Oxford?   _____

Which is the fastest train
from Leeds to Oxford?   _____

You buy a ticket in Nottingham at 9.50.
How long must you wait for
a train to Birmingham?   _____

You need to be in Oxford by 1pm.
Which trains could you
catch from Nottingham?   _____

At how many stations does the
11.25 from Leeds stop before it
reaches Oxford?   _____

18

Test 18 Decimals

Try these calculations involving decimals. Write your answers in the spaces provided, then check them with your number-spotter.

$3.71 + \underline{\hspace{2cm}} = 4$

$2.42 + \underline{\hspace{2cm}} = 2.5$

$8 - \underline{\hspace{2cm}} = 7.35$

$3.7 - \underline{\hspace{2cm}} = 3.63$

What is…

5.175km in metres?   _____

2.35kg in grams?   _____

0.06m in centimetres?   _____

0.4l in millilitres?   _____

450g in kilograms?   _____

1325m in kilometres?   _____

11cm in metres?   _____

4650ml in litres?   _____

Write the decimal equivalent for…

seven hundredths   _____

three thousandths   _____

four and one thousandth   _____

six and five hundredths   _____

eight and one thousandth   _____

Test 19 Percentages

Try these calculations involving percentages. Write your answers in the spaces, then check them with your number-spotter.

What is...

25% of £600?   ———————

40% of 12m?   ———————

75% of 200km?   ———————

30% of 5l?   ———————

80% of 4kg?   ———————

65% of £80?   ———————

Fill in the spaces.

%		decimals		fractions
52%	=	_____	=	$\frac{13}{25}$
34%	=	0.34	=	_____
71%	=	_____	=	$\frac{71}{100}$
7%	=	0.07	=	_____
2.5%	=	0.025	=	_____

A pair of shoes costing £42 is reduced by 20%.
What is its sale price?   ———————

25% of sweets in a bag are green.
If 12 are green, how many sweets are in the bag?   ———————

20

Test 20 Measuring problems

Try these measuring problems. Write your answers in the spaces,
then check them with your number-spotter.

A rosette is made from 75cm of ribbon.

How many rosettes can be made
from 10m of ribbon? _____

How much ribbon is left? _____

A full barrel holds 32.8 litres.
A full bucket holds 4.1 litres.

How many buckets are needed
to fill the barrel? _____

There is 200ml of juice in the small carton.
A big carton holds five and a half times
as much.

How much juice is in the big carton? _____

There is 5kg flour in a bag.
Each cake uses 240g of flour.

How much flour is left when
six cakes have been made? _____

Dan lives 1.4km from the station.
His train journey is 12.9km.
He walks 780m to work.

How long is his journey altogether? _____

I have 6.43kg of potatoes.
I need 8kg altogether.

How many more grams
of potatoes do I need? _____

Test 21 Puzzles

Try these mixed problems. Write your answers in the spaces provided, then check them with your number-spotter.

Find the missing numbers for each sequence.

1.1 2.2 _____ 8.8 _____ 35.2

10 25 _____ _____ 70 _____

1 _____ 9 _____ 25 36

_____ 60 _____ 38 27 _____

−80 _____ −20 −10 _____ _____

What are the missing angles in these triangles?

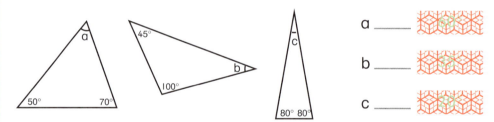

a _____

b _____

c _____

Each of the letters in the sums below represents one of the digits; 1, 3, 4, 6, 8, 9. Work out which letter represents which number and fill in the chart.

A	B	C	D	E	F
4	8	_____	_____	_____	_____

A + A = B   C + C = DB

A x A = DF   A x C = EF

Test 22 Quotients and remainders

Try these division problems. Write your answers in the spaces provided, then check them with your number-spotter. Some have been done for you.

Write these quotients as fractions.

$$85 \quad \div \quad 9 \quad = \quad 9\frac{4}{9}$$

$$67 \quad \div \quad 6 \quad = \quad \underline{\qquad}$$

$$48 \quad \div \quad 5 \quad = \quad \underline{\qquad}$$

$$56 \quad \div \quad 3 \quad = \quad \underline{\qquad}$$

Give these quotients as decimals.

$$307 \quad \div \quad 5 \quad = \quad 61.4$$

$$546 \quad \div \quad 100 \quad = \quad \underline{\qquad}$$

$$213 \quad \div \quad 6 \quad = \quad \underline{\qquad}$$

$$148 \quad \div \quad 8 \quad = \quad \underline{\qquad}$$

What are the missing numbers?

$$87 \quad \div \quad \underline{\qquad} \quad = \quad 14 \text{ r}3$$

$$61 \quad \div \quad \underline{\qquad} \quad = \quad 8 \text{ r}5$$

$$\underline{\qquad} \quad \div \quad 9 \quad = \quad 6 \text{ r}1$$

$$\underline{\qquad} \quad \div \quad 8 \quad = \quad 9 \text{ r}1$$

$$102 \quad \div \quad \underline{\qquad} \quad = \quad 9 \text{ r}3$$

$$\underline{\qquad} \quad \div \quad 7 \quad = \quad 7 \text{ r}4$$

Test 23 Grids

Complete the following questions, writing your answers in the spaces provided. Then check them with your number-spotter.

On this grid how would you write the coordinates for…

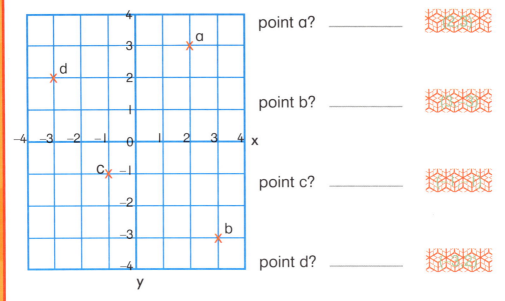

point a? _____

point b? _____

point c? _____

point d? _____

A triangle has the points (0,0), (0,3) and (2,0).

What would its coordinates be
if it was rotated clockwise 90°?_____

The points (−2,1), (−2,−2) and (4,1) are
three of the corners of a rectangle.

What are the coordinates of the fourth corner? _____

A polygon has points (1,1), (1,3), (3,3) and (3,1).

What would be the coordinates
of its shape reflected in the y-axis?_____

Test 24 Money puzzles

Try these money questions, writing your answers in the spaces provided. Check your answers with your number-spotter.

Eggs cost 85p for a box of 6 or £1.26 for a box of 10.

Which is better value? _____

Which is the cheapest way of buying
2 dozen eggs – (A) 4 boxes of 6;
(B) 2 boxes of 10 and 1 of 6; or
(C) 3 boxes of 10? _____

Four friends go to the cinema.
They buy a ticket each, 4 drinks at 80p each and
2 cones of popcorn at £1.30 each.
The total cost is £22.80.

How much was each ticket? _____

24 members of a tennis club go to Wimbledon.
Tickets are £17.50 each. A discount of 20%
is given for groups of over 20 people.

How much money off will the group get
altogether? _____

What is the new cost of each ticket? _____

A house has 2 bottles of milk delivered each
day except Sunday. Each bottle costs 35p.
The bill is paid fortnightly.

What is the cost of milk each fortnight? _____

How much change would there be from £20? _____

How much does the milk cost for a year? _____

Test 25 Mental maths mix

Complete the following questions, writing your answers in the spaces provided. Then check them with your number-spotter.

45 add 216 add 363 _____

multiply 0.4 by 0.3 _____

half of 0.25 _____

3.9 less than 6.8 _____

increase 740 by 197 _____

divide 8 into 168 _____

double 0.55 _____

take 2.6 from 7.1 _____

decrease 1024 by 89 _____

0.6 times 9 _____

72 more than 167 _____

9.3 minus 3.6 _____

425 divided by 25 _____

102 multiplied by 7 _____

subtract 318 from 1409 _____

63 shared by 100 _____

one eighth of 96 _____

2376 times 0 _____

Test 26 Rounding decimals

Round these numbers, writing each answer in the space provided. When you've tried them all, check your answers with your number-spotter.

to the nearest whole number

8.7   _____

23.3   _____

72.1   _____

145.8   _____

to the nearest metre

3.4m   _____

6.2m   _____

4.7m   _____

9.6m   _____

to the nearest £1

£2.57   _____

£11.24   _____

£19.71   _____

£23.18   _____

to the nearest kilogram

1.92kg   _____

5.32kg   _____

Cinema tickets are £4.25 each.
I have £25.

How many tickets can I buy?   _____

How much will I have left?   _____

Test 27 Time problems

Try these calculations involving time. Write your answers in the spaces provided, then check them with your number-spotter.

A hen lays 1 egg each day.
A farmer has 30 hens.

How many days do his hens take to
lay 2310 eggs? _____

How many weeks is that? _____

I buy 3 magazines each month and an
extra one in May and June.

How many will I have bought
between March and July? _____

How many magazines do I buy each year? _____

A plane takes 4 hours 20 minutes to fly to
Turkey. It arrives at 11.10am. There's a
1 hour 35 minute coach ride from the airport
to the hotel. The coach arrives at the hotel
at 1.15pm.

What time did the plane take off? _____

How long was it between the plane
landing and the coach leaving? _____

The times for each lap of a 4 lap
relay race are 14.5 seconds, 17.4
seconds, 15.4 seconds and 14.2 seconds.

How long did the race last? _____

What was the difference in time
between the fastest and the slowest
laps? _____

Test 28 Percentages and fractions

Try these calculations. Circle the answers at the top, and fill in the answer spaces below. Then check them with your number-spotter.

Circle the numbers that are…

$> \frac{1}{2}$	0.37	35%	$\frac{4}{8}$	0.54	$\frac{2}{3}$	45%	
$< \frac{3}{4}$	94%	0.82	$\frac{7}{8}$	0.61	78%	$\frac{2}{5}$	
> 0.33	$\frac{1}{3}$	0.133	25%	$\frac{4}{5}$	0.3	42%	
< 0.25	$\frac{1}{8}$	30%	0.52	12%	$\frac{3}{5}$	0.25	
$> 60\%$	0.8	$\frac{2}{5}$	6%	$\frac{7}{10}$	0.06	16%	
$< 45\%$	54%	0.6	$\frac{1}{4}$	90%	$\frac{1}{3}$	0.54	

Linda made 15 muffins.
60% were eaten at teatime.

How many muffins were left?　　　　＿＿＿＿＿＿　

A bottle holds 1 litre of lemonade.
There are 670ml left in the bottle.

What fraction has been drunk?　　　　＿＿＿＿＿＿　

A bus journey is 5km.
It has travelled 3km.

What decimal portion of the journey is this?　＿＿＿＿＿＿

Test 29 Angles

Try these angle questions. Write your answers in the spaces provided, then check them with your number-spotter.

Estimate the degrees of these angles.

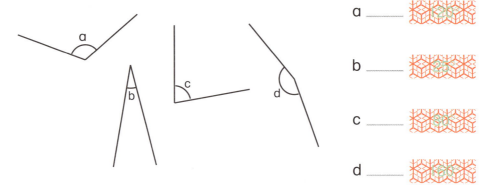

a _____

b _____

c _____

d _____

What are the missing angles of these triangles?

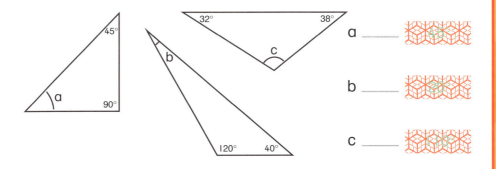

a _____

b _____

c _____

What are the missing angles in these figures?

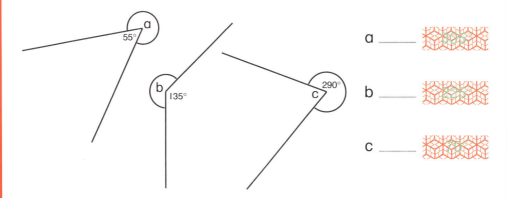

a _____

b _____

c _____

Test 30 Make a number

Find a way to make each of the circled totals from the numbers beside it. (There may be more than one method.) You don't have to use all the numbers. The first one has been done for you.

25   10   10   9   7   5

(253)

$25 \times 10 = 250$
$10 - 7 = 3$
$250 + 3 = 253$

100   10   10   8   7

(682)

50   10   8   6   5   4

(585)

25   10   10   9   8

(492)

50   9   8   7   7   3

(273)

50   25   10   5   2

(650)

100   75   50   25   6

(135)

75   25   6   4   1   1

(494)

Keep your score!

	Score				Score	
	1st time	2nd time			1st time	2nd time
Test 1				Test 16		
Test 2				Test 17		
Test 3				Test 18		
Test 4				Test 19		
Test 5				Test 20		
Test 6				Test 21		
Test 7				Test 22		
Test 8				Test 23		
Test 9				Test 24		
Test 10				Test 25		
Test 11				Test 26		
Test 12				Test 27		
Test 13				Test 28		
Test 14				Test 29		
Test 15				Test 30		